AZIZ HADJ-BOUAZZA

QA IN AGILE: A PRACTICAL GUIDE FOR TESTERS AND MANAGERS

Contents

Chapter 1: Introduction to Agile

1.1 What is Agile?

Agile is a mindset and methodology for software development that emphasizes:

- Customer collaboration over contract negotiation
- Responding to change over following a plan
- Working software over comprehensive documentation
- Individuals and interactions over processes and tools

Agile is not a process, tool, or single method—it is a set of guiding principles that prioritizes flexibility, collaboration, and rapid delivery of value.

Key Characteristics of Agile:

- Iterative and Incremental: Work is delivered in small, manageable pieces.
- Customer-Centric: Frequent feedback from stakeholders ensures alignment.
- Collaborative: Developers, testers, and business users work closely together.
- Adaptive to Change: Teams welcome changing requirements, even late in development.

"Agile is more about mindset than mechanics. It's about delivering value early and often." – Lisa Crispin

---

1.2 Agile Manifesto and Principles

In 2001, 17 software developers came together at a ski lodge in Utah and wrote the Agile Manifesto, which reads:

"We are uncovering better ways of developing software by doing it and helping others do it..."

The Four Core Values:

1. Individuals and interactions over processes and tools
2. Working software over comprehensive documentation

3. Customer collaboration over contract negotiation

4. Responding to change over following a plan

Twelve Agile Principles (a few examples):

- Deliver working software frequently (weeks rather than months)
- Welcome changing requirements, even late in development
- Close, daily cooperation between business and developers
- Continuous attention to technical excellence and good design

For QA professionals, these values shift the focus from rigid test plans to collaborative, adaptive quality practices.

1.3 Comparison with Traditional (Waterfall) Models

Feature	Waterfall Model	Agile Model
Approach	Linear and sequential	Iterative and incremental
Delivery	One-time delivery at the end	Continuous delivery
Change Handling	Difficult and costly	Welcomed and embraced
Testing	After development is complete	Happens alongside development
Documentation	Extensive, upfront	Lightweight and ongoing
Customer Involvement	At the beginning and end	Ongoing and frequent

Example:

In a waterfall project, testers typically begin after the development phase, often discovering defects late. In Agile, testers are part of the development cycle from Day 1, allowing for faster feedback and quality control.

1.4 Agile Roles:

Agile teams are cross-functional. Let's look at key roles, especially from a QA perspective:

Product Owner (PO):

- Represents the business
- Defines and prioritizes product backlog items
- Collaborates with the team to clarify requirements

QA tip: Collaborate early with the PO to clarify acceptance criteria.

Scrum Master:

- Facilitates Agile ceremonies (daily standups, retrospectives)
- Removes obstacles
- Coaches the team on Agile principles

QA tip: Engage with the Scrum Master to raise quality blockers early.

Development Team:

- Self-organizing and cross-functional
- Delivers working software at the end of each sprint

QA tip: Work closely with developers to review code, share test data, and perform pair testing.

QA / Testers:

- Ensure quality at every stage of the sprint
- Write test cases, perform exploratory and regression testing
- Contribute to test automation and continuous integration

The role of QA is evolving—no longer gatekeepers, but enablers of quality.

1.5 The Evolving Role of QA in Agile Teams

In traditional models, QA came at the end of the pipeline. In Agile, QA is embedded into the lifecycle:

Shift-Left Approach

QA activities start early in the development process—during grooming, planning, and design.

Quality is Everyone's Responsibility

QA collaborates with developers, BAs, and POs to define what quality looks like early.

Test Automation and Continuous Testing

QA contributes to automated testing to keep up with frequent deployments.

More Than Just Testing

- Participates in story refinement
- Champions acceptance criteria
- Conducts exploratory testing
- Monitors production health

Key Mindset Shift:

From:

"Let me find the bugs you wrote."

To:

"Let's prevent bugs together."

Summary:

Agile has transformed the way software is built and the way quality is assured. As QA professionals, embracing the Agile mindset means:

- Collaborating early
- Testing continuously
- Focusing on customer value
- Being flexible and proactive

In the next chapter, we'll explore different Agile frameworks and how they influence QA practices.

Chapter 2: Agile Frameworks Overview

2.1 Why Agile Frameworks Matter

Agile is a mindset, but to put it into practice, teams often adopt specific frameworks that provide structure and workflows. While the core values of Agile remain the same, frameworks guide how Agile principles are implemented.

Each framework has its strengths and is chosen based on:

- Team size
- Organizational goals
- Project complexity
- Level of maturity in Agile adoption

For QA professionals, understanding these frameworks is essential for aligning testing practices, communication, and delivery goals.

2.2 Scrum

Overview:

Scrum is the most popular Agile framework, designed for small teams delivering in time-boxed iterations called Sprints (usually 1–4 weeks).

Key Events:

- Sprint Planning: Define work for the sprint.
- Daily Standup (Daily Scrum): 15-minute daily sync.
- Sprint Review: Demo to stakeholders.
- Sprint Retrospective: Inspect and adapt.

Roles:

- Product Owner – prioritizes the backlog.
- Scrum Master – facilitates and removes blockers.

- **Development Team – self-organizing and cross-functional.**

- Participate in all ceremonies.
- Clarify acceptance criteria during planning.
- Perform exploratory, functional, and regression testing during the sprint.
- Contribute to the Definition of Done.
- Help create and maintain automated tests in the CI/CD pipeline.

Tip: QA should start writing test cases or automation scripts as soon as stories are groomed, not after coding begins.

2.3 Kanban

Overview:

Kanban is a visual workflow management framework that emphasizes continuous delivery and flow efficiency without time-boxed sprints.

Key Elements:

- Kanban Board: Visualize work (To Do, In Progress, Done).
- WIP Limits: Restrict how many tasks are in each stage.
- Cycle Time: Measure how long a task takes from start to finish.

QA's Role in Kanban:

- Test stories as they move across the board.
- Ensure testing stages are clearly defined (e.g., "Ready for QA").
- Use metrics like lead time and defects per story to improve process.
- Prioritize test automation to keep up with continuous flow.

Tip: Kanban works well for teams with maintenance, support, or ongoing product work that doesn't fit neatly into sprints.

2.4 SAFe (Scaled Agile Framework)

Overview:

SAFe is designed for large organizations that want to scale Agile across multiple teams and departments.

Key Layers:

- Team Level: Scrum or Kanban teams.
- Program Level: Multiple teams working toward a common goal (Agile Release Train).
- Portfolio Level: Aligns strategy with execution.

QA's Role in SAFe:

- Ensure test alignment across multiple teams.
- Contribute to System Demos and Integration Testing.
- Coordinate with Release Train Engineers (RTEs).
- Drive test automation and performance testing at scale.

Tip: In SAFe, QA often plays a strategic role—governing quality across teams, not just at the story level.

2.5 XP (Extreme Programming)

Overview:

XP is a developer-centric Agile framework that emphasizes technical excellence and frequent releases.

Core Practices:

- Pair Programming
- Test-Driven Development (TDD)
- Continuous Integration
- Refactoring
- Simple Design

QA's Role in XP:

- Collaborate with developers during TDD.
- Write acceptance tests before development starts (ATDD).
- Help evolve the automated regression suite.
- Perform exploratory testing to supplement automated coverage.

Tip: QA in XP must be comfortable with automation tools, and work closely with developers to build a quality-first culture.

2.6 Choosing the Right Framework

There's no one-size-fits-all Agile framework. Selection depends on:

Factor	Scrum	Kanban	SAFe	XP
Team Size	Small to medium	Any size	Large organizations	Small, technical teams
Structure Needed	High	Low	Very high	Medium
Delivery Frequency	Sprint-based	Continuous	Program Increment (PI)	Frequent
QA Collaboration	High	Medium-High	Strategic & Cross-Team	Extremely Close with Devs
Automation Required	Moderate to High	High	Very High	Essential

QA professionals should adapt their test strategies to the chosen framework while staying aligned with Agile values.

Summary

Understanding Agile frameworks gives QA professionals the context they need to contribute effectively. While the roles and ceremonies might differ, the core principles collaboration, automation, quality at speed—remain the same.

In the next chapter, we'll dive deeper into the evolving role of QA within Agile teams not just what we do, but how we think and operate.

Chapter 3: QA's Role in Agile Development

3.1 Traditional QA vs. Agile QA

Traditional QA:

- **Involved late in the Software Development Life Cycle (SDLC)**

- **Focused on finding bugs after development**

- **Rigid documentation and sign-offs**

- **Minimal involvement in requirements or design**

Agile QA:

- **Involved from the beginning**

- **Works closely with developers, business analysts, and product owners**

- **Emphasizes prevention over detection**

- **Embraces automation, collaboration, and continuous feedback**

"In Agile, QA is not a phase—it's a mindset and a shared responsibility."

3.2 Shift-Left Testing

Shift-left means moving testing earlier in the SDLC to:

- **Prevent bugs early**

- **Clarify requirements**

- **Reduce rework and technical debt**

How QA Can Shift Left:

- **Participate in backlog grooming and story refinement**

- **Help define acceptance criteria**

- **Write test cases before development begins (Test-First)**

- **Collaborate in design and code reviews**

Real-world Example: A QA attending story grooming sessions may point out ambiguous requirements early, avoiding future bugs and rework.

3.3 QA as Part of the Agile Team

In Agile, QA is embedded into the cross-functional team. Everyone, including testers, shares responsibility for quality.

Day-to-Day QA Activities:

- **Attend daily stand-ups**

- **Review and refine user stories**

- Write test cases and automation scripts

- Pair test with developers

- Conduct exploratory testing

- Track and retest defects within the sprint

Collaboration Focus:

- With Product Owner: Clarify business needs and test scenarios

- With Developers: Share understanding of requirements and test data

- With Designers: Provide input on UX/usability

- With Ops: Ensure quality in release and monitoring processes

Agile QA = Tester + Analyst + Developer + Advocate for the User

---

3.4 Quality Ownership: Everyone's Responsibility

Agile fosters a culture where quality is not owned solely by QA. Instead, it's a shared commitment.

Ways QA Promotes Quality Culture:

- Define and evangelize the Definition of Done (DoD)

- Coach the team on quality risks and test coverage

- Share metrics and dashboards (e.g., test pass rate, defect trends)

- Run bug bashes or group exploratory sessions

Quote: "Quality is not a department. It's a culture."

3.5 QA and the Definition of Done

The Definition of Done (DoD) outlines what it means for a story or feature to be "complete."

<u>Typical QA-Related DoD Items:</u>

- Code is peer-reviewed

- Acceptance criteria are met

- Test cases are written and executed

- All critical bugs are resolved

- Regression tests pass

- Code is merged and deployed to staging

QA plays a vital role in defining and enforcing the DoD to maintain consistent quality.

3.6 Collaboration and Communication

Effective Agile QA requires constant communication and quick feedback loops.

Key Ceremonies for QA:

Ceremony	QA Involvement
Sprint Planning	Clarify testability, estimate testing effort
Daily Stand-up	Share test progress, raise blockers
Backlog Grooming	Define test scenarios and acceptance criteria
Sprint Review	Help demo tested features
Retrospective	Raise testing challenges and suggest process improvements

Communication Tools:

- Jira or Azure DevOps for test tasks and bug tracking

- Confluence for test documentation

- Slack/MS Teams for quick clarifications

Agile QA must be visible, vocal, and valuable in team conversations.

Summary

QA in Agile is no longer about "checking the boxes" at the end, it's about being an active contributor throughout the sprint. Agile QA professionals must:

- **Shift left and test early**

- **Own quality along with the team**

- **Focus on automation and user value**

- **Communicate constantly**

- **Adapt and collaborate**

Chapter 4: Test Planning in Agile

4.1 Rethinking Test Planning

In traditional QA, test planning is a heavy, upfront process involving long documents like master test plans and test strategy documents. In Agile, planning is:

- **Iterative (revisited each sprint)**

- **Lightweight (no exhaustive documents)**

- **Collaborative (done with the team)**

- **Just-in-Time (aligned with sprint goals)**

Agile doesn't eliminate test planning—it evolves it.

4.2 Components of Agile Test Planning

Even without a 50-page test plan, you still need a clear strategy. Here's what to cover:

1. Scope of Testing

- **What needs to be tested?**

- **What stories or features are in the current sprint?**

- **Are there integrations, UI components, or APIs?**

2. Types of Testing

- **Unit Tests (done by devs)**

- **Functional Testing**

- **Exploratory Testing**

- **Regression Testing**

- **Non-functional Testing (performance, usability)**

3. Tools and Environments

- **Which tools will be used for test case management, automation, and defect tracking?**

- **Are test environments ready and stable?**

4. Test Data Needs

- **What data is needed for testing?**

- **Will mock data or production-like data be used?**

- **Can it be generated automatically?**

5. Test Effort and Timeline

- **What's the testing effort per story?**

- **How will QA work align with sprint timelines?**

6. Risk Areas

- **What features are risky or critical?**

- **Are there external dependencies (e.g., third-party APIs)?**

- **Is there tech debt that could affect test coverage?**

These elements form the basis of an Agile Test Strategy, often maintained in a shared Confluence page or Jira epic rather than a static document.

4.3 Planning at Multiple Levels

Agile test planning happens at different levels:

Planning Level	Activities	Artifacts
Release Level	Align QA with roadmap, identify high-risk areas	Test strategy, scope
Sprint Level	Plan test coverage per story, identify dependencies	Sprint board, test tasks
Story Level	Define acceptance tests, edge cases, test data	Acceptance criteria, test cases

QA should be involved in all levels to ensure coverage and alignment with business goals.

4.4 Using Acceptance Criteria as Test Basis

In Agile, acceptance criteria are the foundation for both development and testing. They define the conditions under which a story is considered complete.

Example:

User Story: As a user, I want to reset my password so I can regain access to my account.

Acceptance Criteria:

1. A reset link is sent to the email address.

2. Link expires after 30 minutes.

3. New password must meet security rules.

4. User receives confirmation email.

How QA Uses This:

- Derive functional test cases

- Build automation scenarios

- Create negative and boundary tests

- Clarify missing or ambiguous requirements

Tip: If acceptance criteria are vague, QA should drive the conversation to refine them before development starts.

4.5 Lightweight Test Artifacts

Agile promotes lean documentation. The goal is to document just enough to guide testing and support collaboration.

Common Agile Test Artifacts:

Artifact	Purpose
Test Checklist	Quick view of what to test per story
Test Matrix	Map user stories to test types (manual/automated, functional/regression)
Exploratory Testing Notes	Session logs with findings
Automated Test Scripts	Living documentation of expected behavior
Bug Reports	Concise, clear, focused on impact and reproduction

4.6 Test Planning and Sprint Workflow

QA must align their work with the Agile development flow:

Agile Sprint Testing Flow:

Before Sprint:

- o **Participate in refinement sessions**

- o **Define test strategy and acceptance criteria**

- o **Prepare test data and environments**

During Sprint:

- o **Test stories as they are developed**

- o **Log and retest defects quickly**

- o **Collaborate on edge cases and automation**

End of Sprint:

- o **Conduct regression testing**

- o **Help with sprint demo preparation**

- o **Participate in the retrospective to improve the next sprint**

Agile test planning is not a phase—it's embedded in the entire sprint.

Summary

Agile test planning is flexible, collaborative, and continuous. Instead of long documents, it focuses on:

- Testing the right things at the right time

- Aligning closely with user stories and team goals

- Promoting visibility and communication

QA professionals in Agile must embrace a lightweight, outcome-focused approach to planning, while maintaining rigor in execution.

Chapter 5: Agile Testing Techniques and Levels

5.1 Introduction to Agile Testing

In Agile, testing is continuous—not a separate phase, but a parallel activity that supports fast and frequent delivery.

Agile teams focus on:

- **Prevention over detection**
- **Collaboration over silos**
- **Automation over repetition**
- **Continuous feedback at every level**

"Testing is not something we do at the end. It's how we build confidence from the beginning."

5.2 Agile Testing Quadrants (Brian Marick Model)

The Agile Testing Quadrants are a useful way to organize testing types based on purpose, audience, and timing.

Quadrant	Purpose	Type of Test	Audience
Q1	Support the team	Unit tests, component tests	Developers
Q2	Guide development	Functional tests, story tests	Team, testers
Q3	Critique product	Exploratory, usability testing	Business, testers
Q4	Evaluate performance	Performance, security, scalability tests	Ops, stakeholders

Key Takeaways:

- Q1 & Q2: Automated and technical—focus on building the product right
- Q3 & Q4: User-facing and investigative—focus on building the right product
- Testing spans all quadrants, not just the end of development

5.3 Levels of Testing in Agile

Agile testing happens at multiple levels. QA collaborates with the team across each of these:

1. Unit Testing

- Written and run by developers
- Fast, isolated, run frequently
- Foundation for Test-Driven Development (TDD)

2. Integration Testing

- Validates how components interact
- Can include API tests, microservices, database layers
- Often automated and triggered via CI pipelines

3. System Testing

- Validates the complete system against functional requirements
- Often black-box testing done by QA

4. Regression Testing

- Ensures new changes don't break existing functionality
- Ideally automated
- Performed every sprint or release cycle

5. Exploratory Testing

- Simultaneous learning, test design, and execution
- Unscripted and creative
- Complements automated tests by finding unexpected issues

6. Non-Functional Testing

- Performance Testing: Can the app handle expected load?

- **Security Testing: Are there vulnerabilities?**
- **Accessibility Testing: Is the app usable for all users?**
- **Usability Testing: Is the app intuitive and user-friendly?**

A strong Agile QA team blends automation with exploration and strategic coverage.

5.4 Manual vs. Automated Testing in Agile

Manual Testing:

- **Best for exploratory, usability, and visual checks**
- **Critical for new features and one-time validations**
- **Should be focused and efficient—avoid repetitive manual tests**

Automated Testing:

- **Critical for regression and continuous delivery**
- **Speeds up feedback loop**
- **Enables Test Automation Pyramid approach:**
-

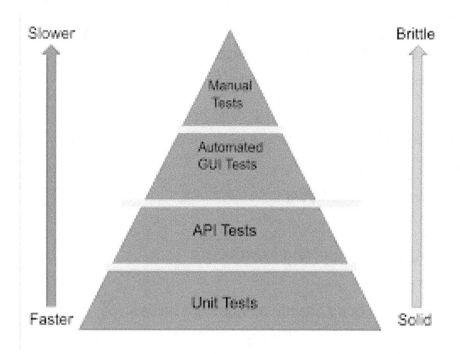

The Test Automation Pyramid helps teams invest their effort wisely—don't automate only at the UI level.

Source: https://automationstepbystep.com/2020/05/02/what-is-a-test-pyramid/

5.5 Test-Driven Development (TDD)

<u>Concept:</u>

- Write the test first, then write code to make it pass.

<u>Cycle:</u>

1. Write a failing unit test
2. Write just enough code to pass the test
3. Refactor and improve

<u>Benefits:</u>

- Cleaner code
- Better design
- Prevents over-engineering

While TDD is mostly for developers, QA can encourage and support it through collaboration and peer reviews.

5.6 Behavior-Driven Development (BDD)

What is BDD?

- An extension of TDD that uses natural language to define tests
- Uses Given–When–Then format

Tools:

- Cucumber, SpecFlow, Behave

Collaboration:

- BDD encourages QA, Dev, and PO to collaborate on test scenarios
- Builds shared understanding before development

Example BDD Scenario:

Given a user is logged in

When they click "Reset Password"

Then they should receive a reset link

BDD creates living documentation of the system's behavior.

5.7 Agile Testing Practices for QA

Practice	Description
Pair Testing	QA and Dev test together, live
Exploratory Sessions	Time-boxed free-form testing
Bug Bashes	Whole team tests together
Mob Testing	Group testing on one device for high-risk areas
Testing Tours	Exploratory testing based on personas or app flows

These practices help uncover edge cases and build team-wide quality awareness.

Summary

Agile testing is broad, deep, and essential to continuous delivery. It covers multiple levels, involves everyone, and balances automation, collaboration, and creativity.

QA's toolkit in Agile includes:

- Unit, integration, system, and exploratory testing
- TDD, BDD, automation frameworks
- Non-functional testing awareness
- Rapid feedback and team alignment

Chapter 6: Test Automation in Agile

6.1 Why Automate in Agile?

Agile teams deliver software frequently—sometimes daily. Manual testing alone can't keep up. Test automation helps:

- Speed up regression testing
- Provide faster feedback
- Support continuous integration and delivery (CI/CD)
- Reduce human error
- Increase test coverage

"In Agile, automation isn't a luxury—it's a necessity."

6.2 What to Automate (and What Not To)

You can't (and shouldn't) automate everything. Focus on tests that are:

✅ Automate	✗ Avoid Automating
Repetitive and high-frequency tests	One-time or rarely used scenarios
Stable functionality	Features still under heavy change
Regression test suites	Tests with frequent UI design shifts
API and backend validations	Complex visual or usability tests

▲ Apply the 80/20 Rule:

Automate the critical 20% of tests that catch 80% of issues.

6.3 The Test Automation Pyramid

Popularized by Mike Cohn, the Test Automation Pyramid is a guide for balancing your automated tests.

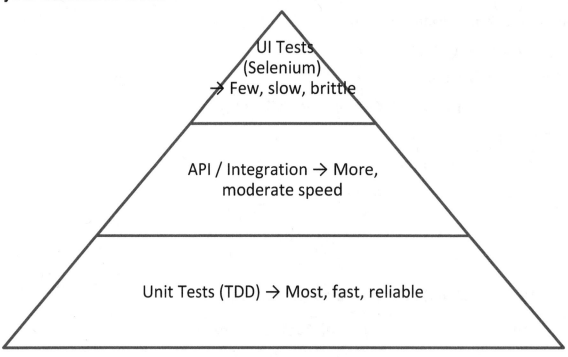

Pyramid Principles:

- **Invest more in unit and API tests**
- **Use UI tests sparingly for critical flows only**
- **Maintain speed and reliability**

6.4 Tools for Test Automation

Common Tools by Layer:

Layer	Tools
Unit	JUnit, NUnit, TestNG, Mocha
API	Postman, RestAssured, SuperTest
UI	Selenium, Cypress, Playwright, TestCafe
BDD	Cucumber, SpecFlow, Behave
CI/CD	Jenkins, GitHub Actions, CircleCI, Azure DevOps
Test Management	TestRail, Xray, Zephyr

Choose tools based on your team's tech stack, skills, and delivery goals.

6.5 Integrating Automation into Agile Workflow

Automation isn't a side activity—it should be part of your sprint.

Sprint Integration Plan:

Sprint Phase	QA Automation Role
Planning	Identify stories with automation needs
Development	Pair with devs on test scenarios
During Sprint	Build and run automated scripts
End of Sprint	Ensure automation is complete for demo/DoD
Post-Sprint	Maintain and refactor scripts

Aim to write automation in the same sprint the feature is developed.

6.6 Automation and Continuous Integration (CI)

Automation is most powerful when triggered automatically using CI tools.

Typical CI Pipeline Flow:

1. **Code Commit**
2. **Build and Unit Test**
3. **Run Integration and API Tests**
4. **Run UI Tests**
5. **Deploy to Staging**
6. **Notify Team of Results**

Benefits:

- **Quick detection of broken code**
- **Team-wide visibility into quality**
- **Fast feedback on every commit**

CI + Automation = Continuous Confidence

6.7 Best Practices for Test Automation

<u>Do:</u>

- **Keep tests atomic and independent**
- **Use version control (Git) for scripts**
- **Use clear and consistent naming**
- **Run tests on clean environments**
- **Automate assertions and validations**
- **Tag and group tests for flexible execution**

<u>Don't:</u>

- **Automate unstable or volatile features**
- **Hardcode test data or credentials**
- **Ignore flaky tests—fix or remove them**
- **Automate just for the sake of it**

6.8 Challenges and How to Overcome Them

Challenge	Solution
Flaky tests	Stabilize waits, avoid UI dependency
Long execution time	Parallelize, split across layers
Maintenance overhead	Modularize code, use reusable libraries
Skill gap	Pair programming, train QA on tools
Environment issues	Use Docker, cloud-based testing environments

6.9 Role of QA in Automation Strategy

QA professionals play a strategic role in:

- Defining what to automate
- Prioritizing tests based on risk
- Creating automation-friendly acceptance criteria
- Reviewing automation reports
- Coaching team members on quality-first practices

QA is not just writing scripts—they drive the automation mindset across the team.

Summary

Agile test automation is:

- Focused on speed and feedback
- Balanced using the Test Automation Pyramid
- Integrated into CI/CD pipelines
- A shared team responsibility led by QA

With the right strategy, tools, and mindset, automation amplifies Agile delivery without sacrificing quality.

Chapter 7: Agile Test Management and Metrics

7.1 The Shift in Test Management

Traditional test management focused on:

- Heavy upfront documentation
- Detailed test plans and traceability matrices
- Separate QA departments tracking everything in silos

In Agile, test management is embedded in the team and adapts continuously. It emphasizes:

- Lightweight planning
- Real-time visibility
- Team accountability
- Continuous feedback

"In Agile, managing testing is less about managing people and more about enabling fast, high-quality delivery."

7.2 Agile Test Documentation

Agile promotes just enough documentation to communicate effectively and maintain traceability without waste.

Common Agile Testing Artifacts:

Artifact	Purpose
User Story with Acceptance Criteria	Defines the "what" and "how" to test
Test Checklist	Ensures story coverage and test readiness
Test Cases (when needed)	For complex or regulated workflows

Artifact	Purpose
Exploratory Testing Notes	Captures observations and unexpected bugs
Bug Reports	Clear, concise, focused on behavior and impact
Automation Reports	Feedback from CI/CD pipelines and test runs

Store test information in tools like Jira, Confluence, TestRail, or Xray—collaboratively and transparently.

7.3 Managing Test Activities in Agile Teams

Integrating with Agile Ceremonies:

Ceremony	QA Role
Backlog Refinement	Clarify acceptance criteria and testability
Sprint Planning	Estimate testing effort and identify test tasks
Daily Stand-ups	Share test progress, blockers, risks
Sprint Reviews	Demonstrate tested features, support PO validation
Retrospectives	Identify process improvements, flaky test cleanups, etc.

Test Task Management:

- Create QA sub-tasks in Jira or similar tools
- Track manual, automation, review, and test data preparation
- Use labels/tags for regression, smoke, or exploratory tasks

Testing isn't separate from development—it's part of delivering the story.

7.4 Agile QA Metrics and KPIs

Agile prefers actionable, lightweight metrics over vanity numbers.

Key Agile Testing Metrics:

Metric	What it Tells You
Test Coverage per Story	Are we covering the acceptance criteria?
Defects Found per Sprint	Bug trends and product quality
Defect Leakage Rate	How many bugs escaped to production
Automation Coverage	% of tests automated for regression stories
Test Execution Rate	How many planned tests are actually run
Cycle Time for Defect Fixes	Time from defect report to resolution
Escaped Defects	Bugs discovered post-release (tracked by severity)

Good metrics drive decisions and learning—not blame.

7.5 Dashboards and Test Visibility

Agile thrives on transparency. QA should make test progress visible to the entire team using real-time dashboards and shared boards.

Recommended Dashboards:

- Defect Trends by Sprint
- Automation Health Reports
- Test Execution Status
- Code Coverage (from CI tools)
- Escaped Defects by Release

Tools like Jira, Zephyr, TestRail, QMetry, Xray, and Jenkins can provide dashboards and reports for sprint demos or retrospectives.

7.6 Defect Management in Agile

Defects are just another form of work in Agile and should be:

- **Logged clearly (expected vs actual)**
- **Prioritized by severity and sprint impact**
- **Tracked on the team board like any task**
- **Reviewed in retrospectives if patterns emerge**

Tips for Agile Defect Handling:

- **Use a lightweight bug report format**
- **Group bugs into themes for better root cause analysis**
- **Encourage team ownership—not just QA responsibility**

"A defect is not just a problem to fix—it's a chance to learn and improve."

7.7 Test Strategy Alignment with Product Goals

Test efforts should align with:

- **Business risk**
- **Customer impact**
- **Technical complexity**

Example:

If a feature involves payment, you may test more thoroughly (including negative cases, integration with gateways, and fraud prevention). If it's an internal tooltip change, minimal testing is needed.

QA leads and testers should adjust test depth based on risk, priority, and user value.

7.8 QA Leadership in Agile Test Management

In Agile, QA leaders shift from command-and-control to coaching and enablement.

Responsibilities of QA Leads:

- Set quality standards and processes
- Define and review automation strategies
- Coach team members on quality ownership
- Ensure tools and environments are working smoothly
- Monitor quality metrics and raise risks early

QA leadership is about building a culture of quality, not controlling testing.

Summary

Agile test management is about:

- Embedding testing into team workflows
- Tracking progress through lightweight, actionable metrics
- Making quality visible and shared
- Managing defects and risk proactively
- Enabling quality through tools, dashboards, and coaching

Chapter 8: Test Metrics and Reporting

8.1 Agile Metrics Overview

Agile emphasizes continuous improvement, real-time feedback, and transparent communication. Key metrics like velocity, burn-down, and burn-up offer visibility into team progress. When coupled with QA-specific metrics, they provide a comprehensive view of both the development and testing efforts.

Agile Metrics: These measure team performance and overall project progress.
- Velocity
- Burn-down Chart
- Burn-up Chart

QA Metrics: These focus on the quality of the product and the efficiency of the testing process.
- Defect Leakage
- Test Coverage
- Automation Coverage

Together, these metrics give you the data needed to adjust the course, plan future sprints, and demonstrate progress to stakeholders.

8.2 Agile Metrics

1. Velocity:

Velocity tracks the amount of work completed during each sprint. It is typically measured in story points or hours, and helps the team understand their capacity for upcoming sprints.

Formula:

Velocity = Total story points completed in the sprint

- Helps predict how much work the team can handle in future sprints
- Adjusts over time as teams become more familiar with estimation

Velocity in Practice:

If the team completes an average of 30 story points per sprint, they will likely complete 30 story points in future sprints unless there are changes to the team or processes.

---

2. Burn-down Chart:

A burn-down chart shows the progress of a sprint, specifically tracking how much work remains to be done.

Formula:

Work remaining = Total planned work - Work completed

- X-axis: Time (days of the sprint)
- Y-axis: Remaining work (story points or tasks)

Burn-down Chart in Practice:

A perfectly linear chart would show the team completing work at a steady pace. If there are large dips or plateaus, it indicates delays or unanticipated issues.

---

3. Burn-up Chart:

While the burn-down shows work left, the burn-up shows work completed over time. This can be especially useful when you are working with changing requirements.

Formula:

Work completed = Total planned work - Work remaining

- X-axis: Time (days of the sprint)
- Y-axis: Total completed work (story points or tasks)
- Shows progress and scope changes clearly

8.3 QA Metrics

QA metrics offer a deep dive into how well the team is managing quality and testing. These metrics help identify areas that need attention and track the effectiveness of your testing efforts.

1. Defect Leakage:

Defect leakage measures how many defects were not detected during the testing phase and were only found after the product went live. This metric helps you gauge the effectiveness of the testing process.

Formula:

Defect Leakage = Defects found after release / Total defects found

Defect Leakage in Practice:

- A high leakage rate indicates gaps in the testing phase or potential areas that were missed during earlier sprints.
- Best Practice: Reduce leakage by ensuring comprehensive testing for high-risk areas and using automated tests to catch regressions.

2. Test Coverage:

Test coverage measures the percentage of the application that is tested. This is a key metric for understanding how well the tests cover the features and functionality defined in the sprint backlog.

Formula:

Test Coverage = (Number of test cases executed / Total test cases) * 100%

Test Coverage in Practice:

- Ensure that both functional and non-functional requirements (like performance and security) are adequately covered.
- 100% test coverage doesn't always guarantee quality—it's about strategic coverage.

3. Automation Coverage:

Automation coverage indicates the percentage of the test suite that is automated. A higher automation percentage typically leads to faster feedback and more reliable regression testing.

Formula:

Automation Coverage = (Automated tests / Total tests) * 100%

Automation Coverage in Practice:

- Start by automating high-risk and frequently tested areas.
- Automation should be part of a continuous integration pipeline to support frequent deployments.

8.4 Reporting Test Progress During Sprints

Transparency is a core principle of Agile. Effective reporting helps stakeholders understand the progress of the sprint, identify potential roadblocks, and address quality concerns early.

Daily Standup Updates:

- QA can provide quick updates on any blockers, progress with automation, and newly discovered defects.
- The team can discuss issues that might affect quality or testing efforts.

Sprint Review (Demo):

At the end of the sprint, the team demonstrates the work completed. QA should:

- Show test results (e.g., number of passed/failed tests)
- Provide a demo of automated test runs (CI/CD)
- Highlight defects found during the sprint (and their status)

Sprint Burndown/Up Charts:

- These charts should be reviewed regularly to check whether the team is on track to complete the sprint goals.

- QA can use this to track progress on test execution and highlight if there are significant delays in testing.

Test Case Execution Status:

- This can be tracked through tools like Jira or TestRail and displayed on dashboards.
- Provide real-time visibility on whether all planned tests have been executed, which tests passed, and which failed.

8.5 Effective Sprint Retrospective for QA Improvements

Sprint retrospectives are essential for continuous improvement. They provide a forum for the team to reflect on what went well, what could be improved, and how processes can be adapted for better quality.

Key Questions for QA in Retrospectives:

1. What went well in terms of testing during this sprint?
   - Did we catch critical defects early?
   - Did automation work as expected?
   - Were we able to test frequently and efficiently?
2. What didn't go as planned?
   - Were there delays in testing?
   - Did we miss edge cases or important functional areas?
   - Were there too many blockers during the sprint?
3. What can we improve for the next sprint?
   - Can we automate more tests to reduce manual work?
   - Are there any areas of the application we should prioritize for better test coverage?
   - Should we improve our communication around defects and blockers?
4. How can we increase collaboration with developers?
   - Did we catch all the bugs in the sprint?

- How can we work together more closely on writing test cases or acceptance criteria?

Actionable Retrospective Techniques:

- Use fishbone diagrams or 5 Whys to dive deep into root causes of issues.
- Implement improvement experiments (e.g., "Let's automate the top 3 recurring bugs next sprint").

Summary

Agile QA metrics and reporting help teams:

- Track progress, ensure accountability, and focus on delivering high-quality software.
- The combination of Agile metrics and QA-specific metrics ensures alignment between team velocity, work completed, and the quality of the product.
- Use sprint reviews and retrospectives to reflect on the QA process and continually improve.

Chapter 9: Continuous Integration and Continuous Delivery (CI/CD)

9.1 Introduction to CI/CD

In modern Agile environments, Continuous Integration (CI) and Continuous Delivery (CD) are critical for ensuring rapid delivery of high-quality software. CI/CD helps teams release updates frequently and reliably, reducing manual intervention and accelerating time-to-market. As a result, QA plays an increasingly important role in ensuring that quality is maintained throughout the CI/CD pipeline.

What is CI/CD?

- **Continuous Integration (CI)** is the practice of frequently integrating code changes into a shared repository, where they are tested through automated tests (unit, integration, etc.).

- **Continuous Delivery (CD)** is the practice of automating the entire process of delivering software to production, ensuring that it can be deployed with confidence at any time.

CI/CD leads to:

- **Faster feedback on code quality**
- **Reduced manual work**
- **Increased confidence in software releases**

QA's role in this process is vital to ensuring that quality is not compromised during fast-paced development cycles.

9.2 QA's Role in CI/CD Pipelines

In a well-established CI/CD pipeline, QA becomes an integral part of the process from the moment code is committed until it is deployed to production.

1. Test-Driven Development (TDD) and CI

QA professionals work closely with developers to ensure that tests are automated as part of the development process. With TDD, automated tests (unit, integration, acceptance tests) are written before the code is even implemented.

- **QA Collaboration with Devs:** QA should review test cases alongside developers during planning to ensure they cover all edge cases, acceptance criteria, and non-functional requirements.

2. Automation in CI Pipelines

Automated testing is the backbone of CI, and QA is responsible for ensuring that test coverage is adequate. QA should:

- Work with developers to automate unit tests, integration tests, and regression tests.
- Ensure that the automated tests run immediately after code commits to validate the latest changes.

The pipeline runs through these stages:

1. **Code Commit** – Developers commit their code to the version control system (e.g., Git).
2. **Automated Build** – The code is built automatically by the CI server (e.g., Jenkins, GitLab CI, CircleCI).
3. **Automated Tests** – Tests are automatically executed (unit, integration, etc.).
4. **Test Results** – The pipeline provides feedback on whether the tests passed or failed.

3. QA in Build and Deployment Stages

- **Build Verification Tests:** QA ensures that there are sufficient tests to verify the build integrity (e.g., smoke tests) at the start of the pipeline to catch basic issues early.

- **Automated Regression Tests:** As the pipeline moves, QA ensures that all the relevant regression tests are included, verifying that new code changes don't break the existing functionality.

- **Performance Testing:** Integrating automated performance tests in the CI pipeline ensures the application meets the expected performance standards.

4. Monitoring Test Quality and Feedback

As part of CI/CD, QA must ensure that the test quality is monitored, with feedback provided as quickly as possible.

- **Test Results Analysis:** Automated tests are run on each code commit. QA monitors the success or failure of these tests and reviews any flaky or failing tests.

- **Immediate Feedback Loop:** QA should ensure that the feedback loop from the CI/CD pipeline is immediate and accessible, enabling developers and testers to fix issues quickly.

9.3 Automated Builds and Testing

Automating the build and testing process is a fundamental aspect of CI/CD. QA's involvement in automating these processes is crucial to achieving efficiency, scalability, and confidence in the product.

🔲 1. Automated Build Process

An automated build process is essential for CI to function properly. QA ensures that this step happens reliably without errors:

- **Dependencies:** Ensure the build process is free of dependency issues and ensure that the correct versions of dependencies are pulled in.
- **Continuous Build Verification:** QA should monitor the build system to ensure it runs smoothly without issues.

2. Test Automation in CI Pipelines

The core of CI is testing, and QA is responsible for ensuring the right tests are automated:

- **Unit Tests:** These are the first line of defense. QA works with developers to ensure comprehensive unit tests are automated and reliable.
- **Integration Tests:** QA verifies the integration of multiple components or systems to ensure they work together seamlessly.
- **API Tests:** QA must ensure that APIs are tested for correctness, performance, and reliability.
- **UI Tests:** While UI tests are slower, automated UI tests can be a part of the CI pipeline for critical user flows.

Tip: Leverage parallel test execution (e.g., using Selenium Grid, Sauce Labs) to reduce the time it takes to run tests.

9.4 Deployment and Post-Deployment Checks

Deployment in a CI/CD pipeline is automated, but QA plays a vital role in verifying that everything functions as expected both during and after deployment.

1. Deployment Process

- **Automatic Deployments:** Once the code passes all tests, it's deployed to staging or production automatically (in a Continuous Deployment setup).
- **Approval Gates:** In some cases, manual approval from QA or stakeholders is required before deploying to production (common in regulated environments).
- **Rollbacks:** QA ensures that rollback mechanisms are in place in case of deployment failures, ensuring that the system can be reverted to a working state.

2. Post-Deployment Checks (Smoke Tests)

After the software is deployed, post-deployment checks ensure that the deployment was successful and that no major issues exist. These checks can be automated as well:

- **Smoke Tests:** Run a suite of quick, high-level tests to check whether the core functionality is working post-deployment.
- **Sanity Checks:** Verify that essential services are running correctly after the deployment.

3. Post-Deployment Monitoring

QA should ensure that the system is monitored for critical bugs or performance issues post-deployment:

- **Error Tracking:** Utilize error-tracking tools like Sentry or Rollbar to catch any errors in real-time.
- **Performance Monitoring:** Tools like New Relic, Datadog, or AppDynamics can be used to monitor the system's performance after deployment.

4. Continuous Feedback and Improvement

QA provides feedback after each deployment to:

- Ensure that the deployed features are meeting quality expectations.
- Monitor the user experience and identify any issues.
- **Retrospectives:** After each deployment, conduct a retrospective to evaluate what worked, what didn't, and how to improve the process.

Summary

Continuous Integration and Continuous Delivery (CI/CD) are vital for maintaining a rapid and reliable software release cycle. QA's role in these processes is to ensure that quality is never compromised, from the first commit to post-deployment. The key responsibilities for QA in a CI/CD pipeline include:

- **Test Automation:** Ensuring comprehensive and reliable test automation.
- **Build and Test Verification:** Monitoring builds and test execution.

- **Post-Deployment Monitoring: Performing smoke tests and ensuring the system is functioning as expected post-deployment.**

With these practices in place, teams can achieve fast feedback, rapid releases, and high-quality software.

Chapter 10: The Future of QA in Agile

10.1 The Role of AI in Testing

The integration of Artificial Intelligence (AI) into the world of Quality Assurance (QA) is revolutionizing testing practices and transforming the role of QA professionals. As AI tools evolve, they can help Agile teams improve the quality and speed of their testing processes, while also enhancing decision-making capabilities.

<u>AI-Powered Testing Tools</u>

AI can enhance test automation by:

- **Smart Test Generation:** AI tools can generate test cases based on user stories, historical data, or business logic. These tools analyze the application and suggest the most critical test scenarios that need to be covered.

- **Predictive Analytics:** AI can predict high-risk areas of an application based on past defect data, allowing testers to focus efforts on areas likely to fail.

- **Automated Regression Testing:** AI can intelligently select and prioritize regression tests, ensuring that key functionalities are validated without having to re-run all test cases.

- **Self-Healing Test Automation:** AI can automatically fix broken test scripts when UI elements change, reducing maintenance efforts.

<u>Machine Learning and Test Optimization</u>

- **Test Prioritization:** Machine learning models can prioritize tests based on code changes and the likelihood of defects, enabling teams to focus on the most impactful tests.

- **Defect Prediction:** AI can be used to analyze historical defect data and predict which areas of the application are most prone to defects, allowing teams to focus testing on the highest-risk components.

Impact on QA:

- **Faster test cycles and higher-quality software**
- **Reduced human intervention in repetitive tasks**
- **Enhanced ability to adapt to rapid changes in software and user behavior**

10.2 TestOps: The Next Evolution in Testing

TestOps refers to the practice of integrating testing into the overall DevOps and Agile workflows in a way that ensures a continuous feedback loop. It extends traditional testing by focusing on improving the test automation pipeline, streamlining test environments, and improving the collaboration between development and QA teams.

Key Aspects of TestOps

- **Test Environment Management: TestOps emphasizes automating the setup and maintenance of test environments. This ensures that tests are always executed in consistent, reliable environments, reducing test flakiness and increasing test accuracy.**
- **Integration with CI/CD Pipelines: TestOps ensures that automated testing is integrated tightly into CI/CD pipelines, enabling continuous testing throughout the development lifecycle. This includes automated tests triggered with every code change, providing immediate feedback to developers.**
- **Test Data Management: Efficient management of test data is a critical component of TestOps. Automated systems can generate and maintain data for various test scenarios, ensuring tests are executed with relevant and accurate data.**

Test Analytics and Reporting

TestOps also includes advanced test analytics:

- **Test Coverage: Measure and improve test coverage using TestOps tools that identify areas of the application not adequately tested.**

- **Performance Metrics:** Track the performance of test automation tools and systems, providing insights into how efficiently tests are being executed and where bottlenecks exist.

Impact on QA:

- Accelerates the testing process by ensuring that tests are executed early and often
- Increases collaboration between development and QA teams
- Ensures that testing and QA practices scale as part of the Agile process

10.3 QA in DevOps and DevSecOps

As organizations increasingly adopt DevOps and DevSecOps, QA's role has evolved significantly. In both environments, QA is integrated into the entire software development lifecycle, from development to deployment and monitoring.

QA in DevOps:

In a DevOps culture, development and operations work together to deliver software faster and more reliably. QA is integrated into this process by focusing on:

- **Continuous Testing:** Ensuring that automated tests are executed continuously throughout the development cycle.
- **Collaboration:** Working closely with development and operations to catch defects early and resolve issues quickly.
- **Shift-Left Testing:** QA gets involved in the early stages of development to define test scenarios, identify potential issues, and validate code before it reaches the testing phase.

QA in DevSecOps:

In DevSecOps, security is integrated into the DevOps pipeline, ensuring that security is considered at every stage of the development lifecycle. QA plays a crucial role by:

- **Security Testing:** QA professionals test for vulnerabilities, security flaws, and potential exploits.

- **Collaboration with Security Teams:** QA works closely with security professionals to incorporate automated security tests and audits into the CI/CD pipeline.
- **Compliance and Governance:** QA ensures that security, privacy, and regulatory compliance are maintained by executing compliance tests and audits during each release.

Impact on QA:
- Ensures a holistic approach to quality, incorporating performance, security, and reliability
- Speeds up feedback loops and improves the quality of the product by ensuring that tests run early in the pipeline
- Enables cross-functional collaboration with developers, operations, and security teams

---

10.4 The Evolving Skillset for Agile Testers

The evolving landscape of Agile, CI/CD, and AI-driven testing requires QA professionals to continuously adapt their skillset. The role of Agile testers is shifting from traditional manual testing to a more integrated, technical, and strategic approach.

1. Test Automation Skills

Automating tests is a critical aspect of Agile QA, and testers must have the skills to create, maintain, and optimize test automation suites. Key automation skills include:
- Knowledge of programming languages (e.g., Java, Python, JavaScript) to write automation scripts
- Familiarity with automation frameworks (e.g., Selenium, Appium, TestNG)
- Understanding of CI/CD pipelines and how test automation integrates into them

2. Data Science and AI in Testing

With AI and machine learning becoming more integral to testing, Agile testers need to understand:

- **AI and Machine Learning Basics: Knowledge of AI-powered tools and how they can be used to optimize testing efforts**
- **Data Analytics: Ability to interpret test data and identify patterns to predict areas of risk or bottlenecks in the development cycle**

3. Collaboration and Communication Skills

As QA roles become more integrated into Agile teams, strong collaboration and communication skills are essential:

- **Cross-functional Collaboration: QA must work closely with developers, product owners, and operations to deliver high-quality software.**
- **Stakeholder Communication: Testers need to communicate test results, risks, and quality metrics clearly to both technical and non-technical stakeholders.**

4. Security and Performance Testing

With the growing importance of security and performance, testers must expand their skills:

- **Security Testing: Understanding common security vulnerabilities and testing for issues like SQL injection, XSS, and other vulnerabilities.**
- **Performance Testing: Knowledge of performance testing tools and techniques to ensure the software meets scalability and performance requirements.**

5. Agile and DevOps Methodology Expertise

As Agile and DevOps continue to evolve, testers need to become proficient in these methodologies, including:

- **Agile Testing: Familiarity with Agile testing techniques like exploratory testing, pair testing, and test-driven development (TDD).**
- **DevOps and CI/CD Pipelines: Understanding the principles of DevOps and how QA fits into the CI/CD pipeline, ensuring continuous feedback and testing automation.**

Summary

The future of QA in Agile is evolving rapidly, with AI-powered testing, TestOps, and DevOps/DevSecOps all playing pivotal roles in shaping the direction of software quality. As the industry continues to embrace these technologies, Agile testers must continuously adapt by developing a diverse skill set that includes automation expertise, AI understanding, security knowledge, and the ability to work in cross-functional teams.

QA will no longer be just a final step in the process; it will be embedded throughout the lifecycle, ensuring continuous testing, feedback, and improvement. Agile testers will become more strategic, collaborative, and technically proficient in delivering high-quality, secure, and reliable software at speed.

Appendices

Appendix A: Glossary of Terms

Here's a comprehensive glossary of key terms commonly used in Agile QA and Software Testing to help readers familiarize themselves with the terminology.

Agile Terms

- **Agile:** A set of principles for software development under which requirements and solutions evolve through collaboration between self-organizing cross-functional teams.

- **Scrum:** A framework used to implement Agile, with roles such as Scrum Master, Product Owner, and Development Team.

- **Sprint:** A time-boxed iteration in Scrum, typically lasting 2-4 weeks, during which a set of features is developed and tested.

- **User Story:** A simple, concise description of a feature or functionality from the perspective of the end user.

- **Product Backlog:** A list of features, enhancements, and fixes that need to be completed in a product, prioritized by the Product Owner.

- **Sprint Backlog:** The set of items from the Product Backlog selected for a Sprint.

- **Definition of Done (DoD):** A shared understanding of what constitutes a completed feature or task, ensuring quality across the board.

Testing Terms

- **Regression Testing:** Testing to ensure that new code changes haven't adversely affected existing functionality.

- **Acceptance Criteria:** Conditions that a software product must meet in order to be accepted by the user, customer, or stakeholder.

- **Smoke Testing:** A shallow, broad set of tests to determine if the basic functionality of the application works.

- **Exploratory Testing:** An unscripted testing approach where testers actively explore the software and discover issues on the fly.
- **Test Automation:** Using scripts and tools to perform tests automatically, as opposed to manual execution.
- **Continuous Integration (CI):** A development practice where code changes are integrated into a shared repository multiple times a day, with automated testing.
- **TestOps:** A practice of integrating testing into the DevOps workflow to ensure continuous and consistent testing, reporting, and improvement.

Appendix B: Sample Agile QA Templates

Here are a few essential Agile QA templates that can be used in real Agile projects.

1. Test Plan Template

Test Plan: A document that outlines the testing strategy, objectives, schedule, resources, and scope for a particular project.

Sample Test Plan Template:

- **Project Name:**
- **Test Objective:** (What are we testing? Why?)
- **Test Scope:** (What's included and excluded from testing?)
- **Test Schedule:** (Test phases, milestones, timelines)
- **Test Resources:** (Team, tools, environments)
- **Test Deliverables:** (Test cases, test results, bug reports)
- **Risk Management:** (Possible risks and mitigations)
- **Approval:** (Who signs off on the plan?)

2. Sprint Checklist Template

Sprint Checklist: A checklist that helps the QA team ensure that all necessary testing activities are completed during a Sprint.

Sample Sprint Checklist Template:

- **Sprint Planning:** Review backlog, prioritize user stories
- **Test Case Creation:** Create or update test cases for new features

- Test Automation: Automated tests created/updated
- Regression Testing: Run full regression suite on all affected areas
- User Story Testing: Verify that user stories meet acceptance criteria
- Performance Testing: Check for application speed and load capacity
- Smoke Testing: Verify basic functionalities before deployment
- Bug Reporting: Log bugs in the tracking tool
- Retrospective: Review what went well, what didn't, and areas for improvement

3. Bug Report Template

Bug Report: Document for reporting defects in the software.

Sample Bug Report Template:

- Bug ID:
- Reported By:
- Date Reported:
- Severity: (Critical, Major, Minor, etc.)
- Environment: (Dev, QA, Staging, etc.)
- Steps to Reproduce:
- Expected Result:
- Actual Result:
- Attachments: (Screenshots, logs, videos)
- Assigned To: (Developer or team responsible)
- Status: (Open, In Progress, Closed, etc.)

Appendix C: ISTQB Agile Extension Syllabus Summary

The ISTQB Agile Tester Extension syllabus provides a foundation for understanding the role of QA professionals within Agile teams. Below is a summarized version of the key topics covered.

1. Agile Principles and Mindset

- The Agile Manifesto and its principles
- The importance of collaboration, flexibility, and responding to change

- Emphasis on delivering value to the customer continuously

2. Agile Testing Practices

- Importance of test-driven development (TDD) and behavior-driven development (BDD)
- Exploratory testing and its role in Agile projects
- Pair testing and collaborative testing techniques

3. Agile Testing Methods

- Integration of testing into the entire development lifecycle
- Continuous testing within CI/CD pipelines
- Managing and prioritizing the test backlog

4. Tools and Automation in Agile

- Importance of automation for regression testing and continuous integration
- Tools for automation (e.g., Selenium, JUnit, etc.)
- Tools for tracking bugs and collaboration (e.g., JIRA, TestRail, Slack)

5. Team Collaboration and Communication

- The role of QA in Agile ceremonies: Sprint Planning, Daily Standups, Sprint Reviews, and Retrospectives
- Collaborating with developers, product owners, and other stakeholders
- Sharing test results and collaborating on improvements

Appendix D: QA Interview Questions for Agile Projects

Here are some common interview questions for QA positions in Agile teams. These questions assess both technical knowledge and the ability to work in an Agile environment.

1. General QA Questions

- What is the role of QA in Agile teams?
- Can you describe the difference between Waterfall and Agile testing?
- How do you manage test cases and test scripts in an Agile environment?
- What is your experience with test automation? Which tools have you used?

2. Agile-Specific QA Questions

- What is the importance of continuous testing in Agile?
- How do you prioritize which tests to automate in a CI/CD pipeline?
- How do you handle defects when they arise during a sprint?
- How do you manage changes to the user stories or requirements mid-sprint?

3. Scenario-Based QA Questions

- You're in the middle of a sprint, and you notice a critical bug in the system. How do you handle it in Agile?
- Suppose the development team pushes new code to the repository multiple times in a day. How do you ensure quality across these frequent changes?
- How would you handle situations when a user story's acceptance criteria are not clear or are ambiguous?

4. Technical Skills Questions

- Can you describe how you would set up an automated test suite for an Agile project?
- What types of tests do you consider essential in a CI/CD pipeline?
- How do you perform load testing and performance testing in an Agile environment?

Summary of Appendices

The appendices provide helpful resources for Agile QA practitioners, offering a glossary of terms to ensure a clear understanding of key concepts, practical templates to streamline Agile testing processes, a summary of the ISTQB Agile Tester Extension syllabus, and sample interview questions to prepare for QA roles in Agile projects.

These resources will support readers in applying the principles and practices discussed in the book and help them excel in Agile environments.

Quiz

1. What is the core principle of Agile?
   - ○ A) Strict adherence to processes
   - ○ B) Flexible planning and iterative development
   - ○ C) A focus on documentation
   - ○ D) Delivering software in large releases

2. Which of the following is NOT one of the Agile Manifesto principles?
   - ○ A) Individuals and interactions over processes and tools
   - ○ B) Working software over comprehensive documentation
   - ○ C) Contract negotiation over customer collaboration
   - ○ D) Responding to change over following a plan

3. What does the term "Agile" primarily refer to in software development?
   - ○ A) A methodology focused on documentation
   - ○ B) A framework for delivering projects through iterative cycles
   - ○ C) A process used in Waterfall development
   - ○ D) The type of project management tool used in development

4. Which Agile role is responsible for ensuring the team follows Agile principles and practices?
   - ○ A) Product Owner
   - ○ B) Scrum Master
   - ○ C) Developer
   - ○ D) QA Engineer

5. Which of the following is a key difference between Agile and Waterfall?
   - ○ A) Agile focuses on rigid phases, while Waterfall is iterative
   - ○ B) Waterfall follows a sequential process, while Agile follows an iterative process
   - ○ C) Waterfall encourages collaboration, while Agile doesn't
   - ○ D) Agile is more focused on documentation than Waterfall

6. Which Agile methodology is most commonly used for software development?

- A) Kanban
- B) Scrum
- C) Extreme Programming (XP)
- D) Lean

7. In Scrum, what is a "Sprint"?

- A) A meeting for project planning
- B) A fixed-length iteration to complete a set of features
- C) A brainstorming session for improvements
- D) A tool used to track project progress

8. Who is responsible for defining the Product Backlog in Scrum?

- A) Scrum Master
- B) Product Owner
- C) Development Team
- D) Stakeholders

9. What is a key principle of Extreme Programming (XP)?

- A) Prioritize customer collaboration
- B) Extensive documentation
- C) Code freezing after each release
- D) Testing after development

10. Which method uses visual management to control workflow and prevent bottlenecks?

- A) Scrum
- B) Kanban
- C) XP
- D) Lean

11. What is the main focus of Agile testing?

- A) To test all aspects of the system after development

- B) To perform a set of tests after a release
- C) To test early and often, within iterations, alongside development
- D) To automate only functional testing

12. Which Agile practice emphasizes collaboration between the Development and QA teams throughout the project lifecycle?
    - A) Test-Driven Development (TDD)
    - B) Pair Testing
    - C) Regression Testing
    - D) End-to-End Testing

13. What does "Shift Left" mean in the context of Agile testing?
    - A) Moving testing to the end of the development cycle
    - B) Starting testing earlier in the software development process
    - C) Shifting responsibilities to developers
    - D) Testing after every release

14. What is Test-Driven Development (TDD)?
    - A) Writing test cases after development
    - B) Writing test cases before code development to validate functionality
    - C) Testing the system as a whole, after the sprint ends
    - D) Writing no tests but focusing on documentation

15. In Agile, what is the role of exploratory testing?
    - A) Automated testing during the sprint
    - B) Writing test scripts for every feature
    - C) Unscripted testing based on the tester's intuition and the product's features
    - D) Documenting all test results after completing the sprint

16. What is the purpose of automated testing in Agile?
    - A) To replace manual testers
    - B) To ensure that tests are run consistently and frequently
    - C) To limit testing to only the most critical features

- o **D) To create a large backlog of test cases**

17. Which tool is commonly used for automated web application testing?
   - ○ A) JIRA
   - ○ B) Selenium
   - ○ C) Confluence
   - ○ D) Jenkins

18. Which type of testing is most commonly automated in Agile?
   - ○ A) Usability Testing
   - ○ B) Regression Testing
   - ○ C) Accessibility Testing
   - ○ D) Exploratory Testing

19. What is the primary benefit of continuous integration (CI) in Agile development?
   - ○ A) Reduces the need for automated testing
   - ○ B) Allows developers to merge code changes frequently with immediate feedback
   - ○ C) Prevents the use of automated tests
   - ○ D) Ensures faster manual testing cycles

20. What is a key challenge when implementing automated testing in Agile?
   - ○ A) Lack of testers
   - ○ B) Integration with traditional waterfall systems
   - ○ C) Constantly changing requirements and code
   - ○ D) Writing documentation

21. In Agile, who is responsible for writing the user stories?
   - ○ A) Scrum Master
   - ○ B) Product Owner
   - ○ C) QA Engineer
   - ○ D) Developers

22. What does "Definition of Done" (DoD) ensure?
   - ○ A) That all tests are automated

- o **B) That the product meets the agreed-upon quality and functional standards**
- o **C) That code is written according to coding standards**
- o **D) That testing occurs only at the end of the sprint**

23. In an Agile team, what is the role of QA during sprint planning?
- o **A) To write code**
- o **B) To review the product backlog and ensure the correct test coverage**
- o **C) To solely focus on test execution**
- o **D) To track progress of tasks in the sprint**

24. Which is a core component of Agile test reporting?
- o **A) Weekly test reports for stakeholders**
- o **B) Documenting every test executed**
- o **C) Continuous feedback and reporting through the sprint**
- o **D) External testing audits**

25. What is the most important aspect of a sprint retrospective for QA teams?
- o **A) Focusing on project delays**
- o **B) Continuous improvement and identifying testing challenges**
- o **C) Writing bug reports**
- o **D) Creating detailed test plans**

26. What is the main goal of Scrum?
- o **A) To complete a project with minimal documentation**
- o **B) To improve communication between testers and developers**
- o **C) To deliver high-quality software incrementally**
- o **D) To ensure that all features are tested after release**

27. Who attends the daily Scrum meeting?
- o **A) Only the developers**
- o **B) Only the Product Owner**
- o **C) Scrum Master and the Development Team**
- o **D) Only the QA Team**

28. What is the Scrum Master responsible for?

- A) Writing code
- B) Writing user stories
- C) Facilitating the Scrum process and removing obstacles
- D) Managing test cases

29. Which Scrum artifact helps track the progress of the work during a sprint?
    - A) Product Backlog
    - B) Sprint Backlog
    - C) Burn-down Chart
    - D) Test Cases

30. What is the goal of sprint reviews in Scrum?
    - A) To plan the next sprint
    - B) To demonstrate the product increment to stakeholders
    - C) To assign new tasks
    - D) To conduct exploratory testing

Answers

1. Answer: B) Flexible planning and iterative development
2. Answer: C) Contract negotiation over customer collaboration
3. Answer: B) A framework for delivering projects through iterative cycles
4. Answer: B) Scrum Master
5. Answer: B) Waterfall follows a sequential process, while Agile follows an iterative process

6. Answer: B) Scrum
7. Answer: B) A fixed-length iteration to complete a set of features
8. Answer: B) Product Owner
9. Answer: A) Prioritize customer collaboration
10. Answer: B) Kanban

11. Answer: C) To test early and often, within iterations, alongside development
12. Answer: B) Pair Testing
13. Answer: B) Starting testing earlier in the software development process
14. Answer: B) Writing test cases before code development to validate functionality
15. Answer: C) Unscripted testing based on the tester's intuition and the product's features

16. Answer: B) To ensure that tests are run consistently and frequently
17. Answer: B) Selenium
18. Answer: B) Regression Testing
19. Answer: B) Allows developers to merge code changes frequently with immediate feedback
20. Answer: C) Constantly changing requirements and code

21. Answer: B) Product Owner

22. Answer: B) That the product meets the agreed-upon quality and functional standards

23. Answer: B) To review the product backlog and ensure the correct test coverage

24. Answer: C) Continuous feedback and reporting through the sprint

25. Answer: B) Continuous improvement and identifying testing challenges

26. Answer: C) To deliver high-quality software incrementally

27. Answer: C) Scrum Master and the Development Team

28. Answer: C) Facilitating the Scrum process and removing obstacles

29. Answer: C) Burn-down Chart

30. Answer: B) To demonstrate the product increment to stakeholders

References

Certifications & Bodies of Knowledge

1. **ISTQB Agile Tester Extension Syllabus**
   - ISTQB Agile Tester Foundation Level
   - Excellent for aligning your book with internationally recognized QA standards.

2. **Agile Manifesto**
   - https://agilemanifesto.org
   - The original declaration of Agile values and principles.

3. **Scrum Guide by Ken Schwaber and Jeff Sutherland**
   - https://scrumguides.org
   - Authoritative for Scrum roles, ceremonies, and artifacts.

Books

1. **"Agile Testing" by Lisa Crispin & Janet Gregory**
   - ISBN: 978-0321534460
   - A seminal book on QA in Agile teams; it introduces Agile Testing Quadrants and real team experiences.

2. **"More Agile Testing" by Lisa Crispin & Janet Gregory**
   - ISBN: 978-0321967053
   - Continuation of the first book with new patterns, tools, and team collaboration techniques.

3. **"Continuous Delivery" by Jez Humble & David Farley**
   - ISBN: 978-0321601919
   - A must-read for integrating QA with DevOps and automation strategies.

4. **"Specification by Example" by Gojko Adzic**
   - ISBN: 978-1617290084
   - Focused on BDD, acceptance testing, and collaborative testing.

Websites & Blogs

1. **Ministry of Testing** – https://www.ministryoftesting.com
   - A top community resource with articles, tools, and tutorials.

2. **Agile Alliance** – https://www.agilealliance.org
   - Deep insights into Agile practices, case studies, and definitions.

3. **Atlassian Agile Coach** – https://www.atlassian.com/agile
   - Visual guides and articles for Agile ceremonies, Jira usage, metrics, etc.

4. **ThoughtWorks Technology Radar** – https://www.thoughtworks.com/radar
   - For trends in testing tools, CI/CD, and Agile methodologies.

Tools & Frameworks Documentation

- **Selenium** – https://www.selenium.dev/documentation
- **Cypress** – https://docs.cypress.io
- **Jenkins** – https://www.jenkins.io/doc
- **Jira/Zephyr** – https://support.atlassian.com